From The Depths
Of My Soul

From The Depths Of My Soul

By

Leevance Williams

Published by
Vantage Point Publishing
3416 N. Shadeland Ave.
Indianapolis, IN 46226

Copyright © 2012 by Leevance Williams

PUBLISHER'S NOTE

All rights reserved: No part of this book may be reproduced or transmitted in any form or by any means, electronic or mechanical, including photocopying, recording, or by any information storage and retrieval system without the express written consent of the publisher.

This book is a work of fiction. Names, characters, places and incidents are either the product of the author's imagination or are used fictitiously, and any resemblance to actual persons, living or dead, business establishments, events or locales is entirely coincidental.

The scanning, uploading, and distribution of this book via the internet outside of the realm of authorized ebook distributors, or distribution via any other means without the permission of the publisher is illegal and punishable by law. Please purchase only authorized electronic editions and do not participate in or encourage electronic piracy of copyrighted materials. Your support of the author's rights is appreciated.

ISBN 978-0-9849630-7-2

Printed in the United States
of America

I dedicate this book to my Savior Lord Jesus Christ, for carrying me when I could not carry myself and for showing me the beauty of struggle. I also dedicate this book to my mother Luretha Williams, for bending over backwards and beyond the call of duty to show me support through out my years from birth. To my kids Albert Antoine, Leevance Williams Jr. and Jada Milord, you have always inspired me through my times of misdirection. To all of the people, the lord felt the need to place in my life through my times of struggle and need, thanks for playing your role. I thank my cousin Felicia Ward and my friend Poetry James for collaborating with me on two great pieces. Last but not least I would like to give thanks to my publishing company for being patient and believing in me. I hope these poetic words, which are taken from parts of my life, impact those who read them in such a way that gives you hope, wisdom and strength. These are key elements that will allow you to push forward through your troubled times. Remember there is no progress with out struggle.

We hear of this great life of sunny days and white picket fences. Well the sun do rise in the morning but it also sets in the evening and the white picket fences, well they are white but they also have to be maintained from erosion due to life's harsh elements.

Through my poetic words of perseverance you will see the beauty of struggle. Someone once said, "Vance, when you make it out of your turmoil, you will be an inspiration and have a great story to tell." This maybe true but I think every one has a story to tell. Don't be afraid to be an inspiration for others. Why be afraid to pick a rose because of its thorns? A prick on the finger is a small price to pay to smell its sweet aroma and enjoy its beauty up close. Never be afraid to push forward because the only failure is to never try at all.

Table of Contents

16 Goodbye

Chapter One:
20 Striving
21 A Brief Prayer
22 A Simple Man's Prayer
23 Age
25 Compromise
27 Happiness and Success
28 I Still Smile
29 If My Struggle Could Speak
31 Inspiration
32 Rain (Collaboration with Felicia Ward)
36 Regret
38 Walking To Work
40 Hope
42 Lord I'm Tired

Chapter Two:
44 Empty Shell
45 Look For Me
46 Friend Stranger
50 Busin It
52 Deception
53 Bogalusa Blues
55 Late Nite
56 Fam
58 We Know Not Our Blessings
60 You Can Make It
62 Sustenance

Chapter Three:
65 Wishing For a Change
67 Wee Hr
68 God Don't Make No Mistakes
69 Punishment
70 Revelations
72 Real
74 Hibernation
76 One Day
77 Solitude
79 Insanity
80 Information
82 The Revolution Is Still On

Chapter Four:
85 Love
87 Inscriptions from the Heart
89 Good Morning
90 Poetry (Collaboration with Poetry James)
94 Confused
95 Heaven Sent
96 A Letter to My Queen
99 No Good Man
102 A Voice
104 Makin Love in the Club

Chapter Five:
109 Thankful
110 A Father's Selfish Ways
112 Those Eyes
114 What Would Have Been Like
116 Dear Mama

118 Good Morning
119 It Lives Within
121 One to Grow On
123 Thank You
124 The End

Goodbye

As I Look Towards The future
My life has been a lesson to me...
Darkness has been my shelter when I felt the need to run, when I thought things were going wrong...
My poetry has been my slave song...
Singing lyrics that kept me coherent thru my weary steps, while building strength thru my perseverance
I have fallen from the sky so many times from flying blind
But just like the moon and the sun creates an eclipse when they become aligned
So has my future, present and past
No more kryptonite!!!
No more games for fame!!
No more excuses and no more people to blame!!!
I am here in the very place where I have been afraid to be...but now!!!
Now I see...it was only me,
It was only me that kept me dangling in the wind...
I no longer have nightmares of a distorted past

I no longer have doubts to make decisions to sustain my present and make a future that will last
I!!!
AM!!!
NO!!!
LONGER!!!
Afraid of my future!!!
There is so much to say!! But more to do,
So I will keep it short…
I!!! …Am …No …Longer afraid of my future.
Imagine going through life…With constant pains and strife
Wondering what the hell is light
And when you finally see it, your so use to darkness that you have become nullified to its beautiful affect to make you blossom…
But I am no longer afraid anymore…I break away from the nocturnal life
I shed the wool, the wool that disguised me as a sheep in wolfs clothing
And now!!!
Now I embrace the mane that has allowed me to obtain the wisdom and knowledge to truly rule my domain!!!

I have evolved into a lion…Wanting!! Needing, to lead my pack of cubs
I have an open heart now, don't know how, but now I feel I can love…
If life causes circumstances to tell Push to relay a message to Shove, I am even willing to kneel on one knee and become submissive to a Queen… with jewels, which can only be seen thru her mentality and sexual immortality.
I wipe the ink from my pen now
I close my eyes and walk as it rolls from the pages it has stained!! You may not see it…but I look back and see al that I have gained……GOODBYE

CHAPTER ONE

Striving

In this chapter I found myself at different times going through the same thing… trying to overcome a sense of spiritual drought, as well as a mental and financial poverty mentality, praying but not fully relying on my higher power to guide me. Eventually as time went on I found myself looking in the mirror stripped bare with only my higher power, myself and a mirror. Honestly, some of us need just only that.

A Brief Prayer

I reach for the sun but will settle for a star...
No matter how distant or far...it maybe,
I still can see my path…
Clear minded and focused, even though I don't know for how long that will last…
I will still!!!
Keep!!!
Striving!!!

A Simple Man's Prayer

All that I have worked for and all that I have gained,
Could be minutes away from going down the drain,
Yet some people still wish for fortune and some wish for fame,
But me!!!
I simply just pray to hold on to what god has blessed me with…
Without!!
Going insane…….

Age

Happiness surrounds me
When I speak my family and friends say,"that's how it sounds to me"…
By weathering through trials and tribulations my Lord and my Savior has crowned me…
Strengthening my belief that angels are constantly around me...
I have been to the bottom of life's disappointments, so... No ONE!!
Can down me!
Naw, Naw, I am at a higher plateau
So stormy troubled tides can no longer threaten to drown me…
And even though my demons still hound me...
I must confess...I have been blessed
To see and overcome each test
So no matter what! They can no longer impound me
I have come from drug addiction...
Judicial restrictions… a stint of homeless affliction

Violent conflictions…Self inflicted death premonitions and Stressful constrictions
Sometimes I thought I had no ear to listen
But yet, I still talked…Sometimes I thought I had no strength…But yet I still fought…
Sometimes I thought--… a person should not be left alone to their own thoughts
But here I am today!!
Same face, same eyes but seeing life in a different way
You see, with age comes growth
With age comes knowledge
With age comes wisdom
With age comes a spiritual devotion
Age is not a number but all of the above
Age is becoming humble and living life with love…And when it's said and done, age will bring you happiness (if you are not learning this then you is not coming up into age)

Compromise

What is it to lose, what is it to gain?
What will make a difference within your boundaries for change...?
What are your limitations to give?
How much more can you endure at the price to really live?
~~~sometimes I just don't know~~~
Do you sacrifice your pride; well it always gets in the way,
Do you admit that you lied; well of course you don't want to make it worse so you turn the other way,
Do you sacrifice what you could be; trying to repair a lost situation,
Knowing you know its time to move on but the emotions that
You're facing, keep lacing your mind with amazing thoughts.
Truth be told I am getting to old for this shit,
It's a bitch! When you do a 360,
Expecting someone to meet you fifty-fifty...
Sometimes it's your fault so you expect the things to come
And things that be,
But it's more frustrating to see!!

That hardship has finally changed you and significant others still disagree,
I leave you with this…a balled up fist and a tooted ass to kiss,
Remember!!...To change for your self, compromising yeah it helps
But it takes two.

Happiness and Success

Happiness and success...
With so much going on it becomes hard to believe or conceive
That it will ever be achieved
Yet I still push on
Striving for the dawn to light my path
Lord forgive me though because I have to ask
Will my load become lighter than yesterday?
I grew up a fighter but I have to say
I am tired!!
I keep my head towards the skies
I keep my soul fed with prayers so it never dies
Through it all my faith carries me along the rough tides
So at the end of the day the sun the moon and my destiny will all coincide,
Because just as the sun rise and just as the moon lights the skies
So shall you light my path for my destiny?
To let me know....how I should get there.

I Still Smile

My motivation within my situation stems from concentration
It stems from the anticipation of success, so everyday that I wake;
I simply just try my best
I ask the lord to hold and guide me thru every test
I guess that's why I feel blessed
Because my lord has never forsaken me
So I smile at the devil cause with my god on my side
He can not make nor break me
People may hate me
But still I am destined to be great you see.

If My Struggle Could Speak

If my struggle could speak
It would bring your attention to the calluses on my feet
The many miles I've walked along the streets
The many bridges I've had to cross to get one inch closer to what I seek
The many disappointments I've had from goals I've fail to reach
As well as the many promises to my kids I've had to breach

But that is only if my struggle could speak
If my struggle could make a sound
It would hold open mic nights on society
Screaming for a life of sobriety
It would be loud like a hungry child filled with anxiety
It would be heard through every ethnic nation that is filled with poverty
Disownment and aggravation
Definitely with the rhythm that has no bounds

But that's only if my struggle could make a sound

If my struggle could make an image
It would look like Langston Hughes, Malcolm X,
Lena Horne, Maya Angelou, Marcus Garvey, Bob Marley
Jacob Jr., Russell Simmons, The Black Panther's movement
It would bare the wrinkles of wisdom
Eyes that have seen hell and back and could camouflage any pain to show, no matter what just keep your head up and keep pushing
A structure that has been chiseled through time and says I'm not limited
And the hands of our fore fathers that show us all if they can do it so can we
But hey that's only if my struggle could make a sound.

Inspiration

I hold my head up so everyone can see it's held up high
So when my day seems like its falling I can still continue to reach for the sky
When the struggle pushes me down I push back with all my might
To let the devil know he can never!!!
Never take away my fight.

Rain

~Collaboration with Felicia Ward~

Rain, please wash away these thoughts
These thoughts that cloud my mind
These thoughts that try to clip my wings from flying
These thoughts that blur my vision, that try to keep me from accomplishing my mission
Rain, please listen!!!
I know you are one of the four elements that sustains life
So thru my strife...am I wrong to imagine as the storm disorients the sands you will situate my strife
Just like how the sand looks after your storm in the morning light.
<Felicia ward>
Rain on me, for I will love the sun more when it shines
Rain on me, for I will be cleansed when this storm passes
Rain on me, for it will wash away the grime and grit and grunge that fill me, so that when the sun comes
I am refreshed!!
Refilled!!
Reborn!!

Rain, I beg you rain on me!!
Wash me clean, flush my mind, flood my thoughts so that the lovely sunshine, when it comes….oh when it comes
What a blessing

<Leevance Williams>
And when the sun decides to come
I will know my storm has finally passed
Giving strength and renewing my faith
Leaving only one trace of a battle and I am sure you would appreciate and embrace
A thankful stream of tears….running down my face

<Felicia ward>
While you wait for your storm to finish passing
I feel you gathering your will for the new day
I see you ordering your steps to go a new way
Thinking and doing things for faith more lasting
And embracing that rain for the strength that it gave

For the power to embrace the light that will save
I see laughter and joy, no tears on your face!
Go forth young man, take this happiness, and embrace!

<Leevance Williams>
And embrace it I shall...you see it can't rain everyday so I know this storm won't last
I know by faith and by the word that the good lord will shelter me while it passes
A lot of people walk up to me with curiosity and ask
How do you smile when it seems your going thru a test?
I simply say…
I am at my best…when my back is against the wall
Because no matter what I am still blessed, the sound of the thunder in the sky helps me stand tall
To some that lightening is frightening!!
But its music to my ears
Only god can produce such power
Or should I say!!... My god!!
And the fear I have is respect so all the while!!

This is why I still smile!!
Because if he can make it rain and make it thunder
He will see me thru my quest of elevation, so indeed I will embrace it like the power of gravitation.

Regret

His life goes from dark to light
Light to dark
God knows his heart and his fight
But what good is that if he can't play his part and do what's right
He tries so hard with all his might to stay true from the start, but its like
It's hard to keep sight
When your dreams are slowly being consumed by the darkness of the night
I got to give it to him he walks proud like a four star general who has earned his stars and stripes
By battling so many thoughts of his faults with no gripes
He takes hand and looks towards the sky and mimic wings that take flight
Thinking that's far as he will get because his own will never reach that height
He holds a photo glass frame of his kids with delight
Grip so tight!!
That he shatters the glass, thinking to himself how they grow sooo fast

Wishing he would have paid close attention while in class
Now he is left with one achievement that falls far from grace
A disappointing expression…every time, he looks…In his child's face.

Walking To Work

Every morning to work I walk…gracefully…with pride
Graciously …my stride...hides, the feelings and emotions that calls for help
I try not to be so ungratefully for self
So I keep my chin up and hold down my cries and my whelps
I keep my eyes filled with strength…at least the little that is left
I watch cars pass me by with optimistic drivers wishing that was I… quiet is kept
Back in the days I would have made them know how I felt
But today I try to stay humble and continue my journey
I see doubtful looks as they scurry to their rich society coffee shops...I pause-------
And as I continue to walk by sometimes I have this premeditated plot
But then I have to forcefully tell myself...STOP!!
You can't think of self!!
Still walking…talking to myself
Wishing I could win that lottery

How miraculous the change of my spot would be
Hell!! At least that's what it would seam
But I quickly snap out of it because it's only a dream
Finally! I step into a world filled with attitudes… souls in a fast lane to make that doe in great magnitudes
But you should see their faces when they get their checks
Slowly they decline…
I can't even lie! …I am not special so do mine
Who ever said a penny turns into a nickel…a nickel turns into a dime and so forth on!!
They should have left well enough alone!
You see in my world…a dollar turns into a quarter...a quarter turns into a dime and a dime turns into a nickel
Yeah in the beginning it looks like plenty
But in the end
You will be lucky to save a penny
This is just my thoughts…All along the journey….
Walking To Work

Hope

She is bestowed upon me every time I am able to open my eyes
She is given to the world every time a newborn baby cries
But she becomes hard to carry every time she is defied...
By her twin brother despair
I sometimes question her and ask..."Is it fair?"
Is it fair to watch those that don't care become millionaires?
Is it fair to watch a person with such greed...progress off those who need?
Yet, for some reason she still gives me strength to proceed
At one point in my life I thought she had died
But there eventually I found her healthy and alive...still on my side as I struggled and strived
Seven though sometimes she was disguised but who said her DNA is easy to decipher
She talks with me and takes long walks with me
She advises me that her very essence is given from the heaven if you seek it

It cost nothing to have it…but it takes a fight to keep it
It takes a devoted humble heart to grab it and an ignorant individual to say", who needs it."
Me myself hell! I am married to her
We have renewed our vows time and time again
Matter of fact! She has become my best friend
She has carried me through rough tides, rough weathers, long cries and disappointing endeavors
Who am I to turn my back?
Who am I!! Not to compliment her and stay on track
Who!!...Am!!...I?
She even helps with that
After every year of my devotion she helps me define myself
She is wonderful
She is my life line
And when I am falling she throws me a rope
I just don't know what I would do with out her
My friend…my HOPE

Lord I'm Tired

Today I wake confused
Abused by the thought of me paying dues never paying off
Tired of walking like a zombie trying to play it off
Tired of wearing this make up, I just want to take it off
They say it's ok if a grown man cries…but hell!!
People tell a lot of lies…
So I will keep my tears and my fears to myself…kneel and pray and ask for help
Because to me a grown man depends on the lord, himself and no one else…to survive…But lord!!!I can't lie…I! Am! Tired!!

CHAPTER TWO

Empty Shell

In this chapter I found myself thinking of a means to an end. I found myself at my lowest point seeing things from a different point of view; literally I was outside looking in. I can't speak for every one except me but honestly with the foot prints that I was leaving in the sand, it was a place that help me find myself and god. A place that help me realize my strengths and motivation, as well as help give me a chance to deal with and forgive myself and let go the burdens I carried.

Look For Me

2 thousand pennies
To some may not be much but to some it is plenty!
It could get me an all day pass to ride the chariot around the whole city
If I save it 45 more times I can get up to fifty
Don't get me wrong I know saving 2 thousand pennies won't get me there quickly
But even the biggest body builders started off lil bitty
I keep my 2 thousand pennies tucked away in my pocket like it's an unknown secret
Shhh! Don't tell the man in the mirror or I might not be able to keep it
I feel strange, I been feeling a growl all day
Thought it was the man next to me on the bus, he looked hungry; I didn't really want to say
It's funny because as I passed convenient store windows, I saw this man time and time again
Shit if a stranger would have watched us they would have swore he was my friend

I reached in my pocket and grabbed a list filled with jobs
And you know what, it was kind of odd…it's like I said the magic word for him to disappear
With nothing to fear, I eased on down the yellow brick road, only there was no oz to grant me an employment wish
With frustration in my face and tension in my fist!
I said well at least I can go get a sandwich and brush off today's defeat…
Reached in my pocket and my dam 2 thousand pennies said look for me!

Friend Stranger

She came to me at a time when the word lost meant...
Living Outside Trapped,
I was pretending
But as she kept listening
She felt the trail of my words
Outside its tracks, de railing and failing to live up to the sounds of laughter I portrayed,
She was amazed
Amazed by the strength it took, to keep up this look
She played along; only to help me string that difficult happiness song…that evidently got me thru the day.
Consequently, it wasn't that hard to hear strings popping in each verse
Every other word cracking and stopping,
Trying not to let her see my pain!! The hurt!!
Once separated all I could do was curse!!(FUCK!)
But soon as my friend stranger communicated again
It seemed all the sadness came to an end

And a philosophical connection began
Giving strides to my weary steps
Unveiling all that I disguised, saying god is on his way, trust me he will help
It's funny because all my life I have seen statues… of angels
But none that gave me more gratitude…like this voice
Never were their faces painted with color
But this one was BLACK!!!!
I can tell from the lingo of her tongue
The known struggle in her wisdom
I could tell by her tenacity, that there was no question how black she is.
You see because I could feel her wings sheltering me from 1,000 miles away, almost like a Hebrew slave protecting her child from the sting of the whip
LET DAT MARINATE, WHILE I HOLD UP MY BLACK FIST!!
She told me she would pray for me but I had to ask...
How can another stranger pray for another stranger to be safe and out of danger?

A concept I couldn't fully grasp hold on to...
She said, "POPPI",
Oh by the way that was another reason I knew she was black with a warrior mask
She said, "You and I are one, this struggle you're going through, my feet has been just as deep."
"The darkness you see, at one time, my eyes saw darkness just as bleak."
"The loneliness you feel all you got to do is just kneel"
"That is why I can pray for another. Who am I to receive his blessing and not pass it on?"
"All you got to do is believe and stop second guessing."
Her words penetrated me and cut me deep down to the bones
Leaving me with a Jones, like a fiend for another hit
So here I am staring out the window
No pity, No more tears, No more fears
Not even an ounce of anger...all due to...my...FRIEND STRANGER.
(Dedicated to you BORICUA)

Busin It

She stood next to me as we waited for our diesel chariot, eating jalapeño chips… I could smell them in the air, I kind of felt it was unfair because my stomach was rumbling more than the thrilla in manila.
I hear a female in the bathroom singing melodies of struggle, yet brown skins criticize, when they barely have a dollar for fare
Old heads watch big asses pass by…stuck in a jack the ripper stare
Lil man dragging a cooler filled with chips and other morsels for the ghetto sweet tooth...Guess we all got to make a living
Guess we all can't be like Michael Bivins selling poison
The cold air whipping by as the chariot passes by…DAMMM!! I can't lie...That hawk got my knees

knocking like a 57 Chevy with no oil!!
Awww shit!! This dude did not ask me to move over to camouflage his ghetto pharmaceutical sale!!
Man!! I am on papers!! So all I can hear is LL rock the bells…but I just move to another seat singing, Otis Redding, "One day A Change Gone Come".
The Chariot switches lanes and I'm at my destination…stepping off smooth like my name is CAT! DADDY!!... chin up high …but I be damn if that hawk didn't remind me of who was cool when it breezed on by…Shhhh yeah I fumbled wit that zipper but I wasn't to shy… I eased down my path making it to my honey comb hideout…Resting my bones thinking about tomorrow's grind so I attentively sat…feeling a cool breeze I thought...Well I be John Brown!!!!!
I left my dam skull cap!

Deception

I'd rather close my eyes and not see the repercussions of all my lies that I have told
To try to somehow shield me from all the short comings, that leaves me bare and cold…
To try to some how get over the fact! Of how childish I may act…yet becoming so old...
I'd rather close my eyes…
Then to face that role, of a father that has been bestowed upon me…
I guess I mistaken the darkness to take it all away…
But at the end of the day... When I close my eyes, no matter what I may say…
I see them even more!

Bogalusa Blues

Conscious thoughts turn into the unconscious wishes to see light again…
Wishes to be able to write again…
The strength to be able to go head up with life and fight again…
I even wish to sin again, with the love of my life…
Opening to a sight that bares no hope for human rights…
Strapped down with tubes in my body…Watching all the who's who surrounding me…
Vision cloudy like the truths of illuminati…dealing with dangling thoughts from the following night has left me damaged like pressured pipes…
My actions have left me unable to deal with the repercussions that have come at a costly price…
One that has left me to be evaluated, one that has DE gravitated my present life…
One that may have decapitated the rest of my life…
Aggravated!!...By the burdens of be unsuccessful…
Constipated!!...By the every day bullshit…

Desperately trying to reason with my own selfish reasons, to leave my love one with o father…
No brother…
No son…Or no lover
Tired of keeping my mental struggle under cover…
So here I am singing the Bogalusa Blues to a sad tune behind screen windows…if only I could have seen such events…Maybe I did but didn't pay attention…
Now I am left to death defying thoughts of the revival of myself while clenching, to my life...
Louisiana lynching!!
But in this story it's by the hands of a black man.

~~DEATH IS NOT AN OPTION FOR LIFE~~

Late Nite

In the midst of my sleep I awake!
These DAM! Burdens that I carry like clock work torment me to wake
Thinking about all the opportunities I took and the ones I today with no thought that I rape
Not just the ones that are blessed and given to me but also the wrongful ones that I try to hurry and make
I see how far I fall from grace…when I pray I ask the lord is it too late?
Is it too late for me to correct those wrongs before my expiration date?
I know he answers me, but deciphering his response is not one of my better traits
But I still have faith that my soul he will take.

Fam

Family...Well it speaks for its self...Sometimes they love you at your best...But other times they don't know you when life sends you through its tests...but blessed- be the one that upholds the saying, "I Am my brother's keeper.
Who cant say when times are difficult to smile...that there is nothing in the world like picking up a phone to dial...Good ole fam!!
All I can say is….DAMN!
How many know what it feels like to be alone...how many know what it feels like to be disowned...how many know how it feels to just roam, with no one to talk to...with no one to walk with but you...its hard to not have fam!
All I can say is...DAMN!
When you need advice...when laughter doesn't suffice...when darkness

seems to overcome your life…there is nothing like!
FAM…
Let's say it together…
DAMN!
DAMN!
DAMN!!

We Know Not Our Blessings

I watched as he dug in through the trash bags, within the downtown streets…Looking for sustenance to help him shuffle across the concrete jungle

I can tell from the facial mask that he had lost all hope in society...But he still believes there is a god because he found a chicken bone half eaten

I watched as he moved through the crowd of business suits getting degrading looks…but they never penetrated his soul…Because every look he received, he still walked strong like a slave who has been striped of his clothes…yet still maintaining his honor.

I watched as he held his hand out asking for a spare dollar…protect and serve asking him to move on, no soliciting instead of reaching in their own pockets

Protect and serve…Protect! And Serve…a joke many of us has heard

I watch as he continued his journey turning up his thin jacket

collar to help warm his old malnutrition bones
I watched…I watched…
All of a sudden he turned around and he stared at me, as if he knew I was watching
I gave him my last dollar…he looked at his hand and looked at me…slowly he said, "Son...God told me to tell you keep your dollar…you need it more than I".

You Can Make It

Sleeping in a vacant hallway listening to the raindrops washing away the old year on new years day
My lips have few words to say…but my mind is on cue with over due words to say
How did I find myself in this position…you would think before shit got thick I would have taken a small intermission…before things started constricting
Now here I am christened, in the name of hard times
I tell myself, "I can get through this, I am not new to this."
So I put one foot ahead of the other…never looking back…never holding regret…always walking with my head held high…never losing myself respect
Never forgetting the smiles on my seeds face…eradicating every single trace!-of a broken soul, but always keeping in sight of what tried to break it
Of who tried to take it and who watched over me and kept me safe and showed me how to save it

Keeping in mind what my mama called me and said, "Son I believe in you, just have faith, You Can Make It!"

Sustenance

Head held low...strength so weak...it didn't take a rocket scientist to understand why it spoke to me
My steps were ones of a lion stalking its prey...lord forgive me is what I started to mumble and pray...if my mother could see me I wonder what the hell she would say...But the feeling was so strong I though I wouldn't last another day
I circled around as I felt all eyes on me, to paranoid to see...that no one paid attention just thought thru my nervousness they would know
But hell it could have been a million people in that spot, it still wouldn't have stop this show
It cried to me and I cried to it...for it was the tears from last night's growling that had me so committed to this shit
Lord I know its wrong and this is something I already know...but last night felt so long that I woke knowing what I was already going to do
Soft white bread with succulent dark meat... up under my jacket and

swiftly I walked out the automated doors with out skipping a beat
I unwrapped it… as I unwrapped my presents on Christmas day…and even though it was born and committed in sin I still bowed my head to pray
Lord forgive me for what I have done, please don't allow this sin to pass down to neither one of my sons
Forgive me for indulging in the ungodliness of the world and may my action not touch the purity of my dear little girl
As I held it…I asked myself, "Is this what you have become, a man with no morals, a man settling to defeat!"
DAMMIT!!!
I lost my appetite listening to reason and that dam roast beef sandwich I wanted to eat!

CHAPTER THREE

Wishing For a Change

In this chapter I began to learn more about myself. I began to realize who's in my corner and to learn more to rely on my higher power to guide me. I must admit I still questioned things and why. They say if you truly rely on your higher power then you wouldn't question it. Well I am here to tell you we are human and by nature we are curious. So yes there will be times you will question it because you may feel you are doing what it takes to improve your situation but yet and still it is not going right. The difference with that is your question should come in the form of a request. Ask your higher power to give you understanding of why. I also began to come into my growth stage from enduring my trials and tribulation. Let's get something straight I do not mean I began to become a perfect person, simply a person better than yesterday. My mind began to process my trials in a different view; I began to give thanks more often even when it was not going right. I began to talk more to my higher power and ask for help than to rely on self. Above all this point was when; you can say I began to think more like a man.

Wee Hr

Its 4:19 and I am laying in my bed
With my eyes open...hoping...that these
Thoughts in my head that are
Frightening...would stop sticking
Like lightning in a bad storm...
They say in the midst of it you
Must be calm...so I ball my fist up
And wait for the dawn.

God Don't Make No Mistakes

I take no orders except from god
And if I do its only because it allows my odds…more acceptable to achieve my goals
A wise woman name Luretha once told me, "Son you get out of life what you put in it and before you finish…tears will fall but so will the walls of fear".
But let's be clear!
The path you try to steer…it will never be easy
Hence the hence the saying, "Anything worth having is worth the work".
Hence the loud clapping…when a graduate strolls to get that document that unfolds the rest of their life
This leaves me with knowledge and endurance to do what it takes
Because no matter how hard the struggle
REMEMBER!!!
<<GOD DON'T MAKE NO MISTAKES>>

Punishment

What can you expect from them…after you bring such disrespect to them…after the few rules and devotion to them you just neglected of them?
It's sad because it still hurt when I reflect on them…I though the worst could dissect the worst as long as I had my best friends
But my action said another
Not many know these are a blessing to them…now I am left to walk life with just make up to blend…
Guess it's my punishment for taking you all for granted

Revelations

The more my life starts to get short like a wick on a candle
The more it twists and turns into shambles
The more I encounter things that become hard to handle
The more my life seems so unfair to my dreams…the more I start to see things
Like the interference of my own mind…the hindrance of my own kind and the outcome of a race that becomes blind
The more my life takes on casualties…the more I pray to hold on to my soul through out my tragedies
Because with so many persuasions…that is the only thing that connects me to eternal life…through spiritual resuscitation
The more life seizes to exist…the more I clench my fist and try to

resist...The emotions from not being prepared

You see my life has been like a roller coaster with no destination…and though a lot of it has been my fault from falling into temptation

I just kneel, pray and take a stand…ask for forgiveness and wash my hands…then I am renewed with a new found strength to start once again

Now days... the more my life opens up I see it more like a book in history…not a mystery

But more of a revelation of some sort

Every year is a page number every month is a chapter and everyday is a lesson

The more my life gets closer to God the more I see the end of this book as it is already written

Take a moment and just listen…and as you hear and feel these words…watch how clear and real these words

Will allow you! To see it too!

Real

Real!
Real is waking up in the morning with hunger pains…filling out applications wondering if the effort was in vain
Real is when all you can do is pull out of your pocket is 100% cotton, while sitting on your sofa contemplating and plotting
Real is when a woman's eyes is purple and she tells her friends, "Girl he just under pressure".
Real is a crack fiend with a pipe in one hand and a hand full of crack in the other saying, "lord I am blessed". (Go figure)

Real is an everyday test that life sends you thru constantly weighing on your beliefs and faith …
The strength to over come, God gives us all that entire trait
But some don't know how to humble themselves to sit back and wait
Real is when a child feels like he is growing up to be a man all by himself…the father to selfish to

give him help…so he turns to the streets because he feels he has nothing left
Real is when all odds are against you but still manage to succeed
Real is no matter how bad you bleed…You pick yourself up and wipe off your knees
Real is giving thanks to the good and the bad times…you see I would be lying if I didn't say, "Real! Is a muthfucka!"…but simply reality
I don't know about your, Real< but my own!!
Well it simply involves me trying to evolve into who I am supposed to be.

Hibernation

Today I wake from hibernation…born a new creation
All of my sinful past has been shed like sheep's wool that once covered my eyes…and to my surprise…I look in the mirror in see a new image that has been reshaped and reformed...Like the rain does the sand after every storm
My eyes are blurred from the ability to see things more clear
My language sl>>urred...From speaking the truth for so long
My mind…free as a birrrd…from being locked up and confined with no place to roam
My senses are awaken and amplified, no longer nullified by the coldness of the world
My steps are slow and weak, like a newborn child but steady and careful like a man with wisdom
My soul…Explosive!!...Warm!!! And vibrant like the birth of a sun

My posture strong and erect like a Hebrew slave no longer on the run
But as I see my aura shining bright like the heavens… a tear drop falls like condensation…and I realize!
It's a beautiful thing…
To awake… from HYBERNATION.

One Day

I swear it seems like everyday I
Wake to an obstacle…but I
Constantly tell myself giving up is
Not optional and even though
Sometimes it seems impossible
I just grit my teeth and move my
feet to the rhythm of the drum
Because I know one day!
A change gone come!

Solitude

Give me life or give me death
How much more pain shall I feel through my inner soul of self
Stuck In a realm where I have exhausted all of my help…now left alone to feel the pain, three times fold felt I feel it through every turn, through every step
Not from the lack of knowledge
Not from lack of wealth
But from the lack of love and the lack of respect
Over time it has caused a dramatic drop in my health
I stare through a window and even though it sheds light
I still can't feel the warmth from the sun no matter how hard I fight
Maybe because I never wanted to make a sacrifice
Always having others sacrifice themselves for me…but eventually
I learned that greed and selfishness made it hard for me to see…that my own thoughtless acts hindered me from being who I was born in this world to be

I pray and ask the lord to give me sight...to one day be able to look in the mirror and see a person whom I like

No more temporary steps that last only an hour...no more settling for less for choices that only implode and devour

No more not setting goals that allow chemicals and people to intrude

And definitely!!

Fuck anything and everyone that cause me to be in...SOLITUDE!!

Insanity

Insanity, is when you have the key to unlock that lion you have inside but to scared to push and strive…to scared to go that extra round…that extra bout…to scared if you need to kick, scream or shout, to absorb that energy and let the beast out…if need be scream with the last breath in your lungs, til the back of your throat becomes numb…Haven't you heard only the strong survives…if so…fear no man, clear your mind, ball your fist and stomp your feet…because

battles are won by being wise and strong and not by being self centered, selfish…ignorant nor weak!

Information

Information
Something our culture needs to survive the system that subject us through segregation and degradation
It's more political today…you need this to overcome accusations
INFORMATION
Something we as black men need who dwell in the bowels of the street…constantly subjecting them selves through litigations…make a notation my brothers…you need this to find your destination
INFORMATION
Something our woman need to push through life's unfair frustrations…to forget those limited minds who think you all have limitations…forgive them my sisters it's an illness derived from mental starvation(ignorance)
INFORMATION
Something we as a whole need to pull together and become kings and queens of this nation…I don't know about you but my president been black every since my mother taught me how to pray…so lets plant and nourish our seeds through proper

cultivation…taking a strong initiation…to pick the next man up, keeping a proper rotation…because when you are old and grey, you'll be glad you stuck with it……
INFORMATION.

The Revolution Is Still On

Many of us commit ourselves to correctional institutions…born in the very pollution that breeds a militant mind

Bureaucratic wars are now camouflaged within our communities…creating blind folds that separates our unity…which eventually leads us down pathways we never dreamed of having

Leaving us baffled weak and staggering with burdens we never dreamed of having

So we commit genocide because we are put into position to give a violent contribution. But if we would only be calm and listen…we would find a better solution…but instead we turn to ignorance…a diligent destructive affliction…that leaves no hope just restrictions…no open minds, no better way of living…so many of us are left to the chemical controlled addiction

Giving reason for the practice of immoral laws …leaving us pleading for that minimum action that leaves your life on pause…but for some of ya'll, it leaves no life at all

Now tell me do you fight for the revolution…a constant struggle for retribution…you see with out no cause you're just an expendable asset…dependable for drastic tactics…to embody funeral caskets…becoming part of a blue print that lay fallen soldiers

But you see the revolution will never die…it only multiplies backbones that stand firm as red wood trees…souls that wont burn because we are destined to be free!

Now tell me!

Do you fight for the revolution or do you fight for the cause that practice immoral laws.

CHAPTER FOUR

Love

In this chapter are pieces that explore the years that I thought I found love and years when I found my true love, POETRY. Sometimes we don't understand that when we meet someone they are not actually there for a long term relationship or even a relationship period. We as humans sometimes think with emotions and screw up the blue print that has been laid down for our teachings and life. I can say this; people are put into our lives for reasons. This is also when you rely on your higher power to give you the reason for this before you take it upon yourself to decipher it for your own selfish reason. Life is filled with love and pain, so to have experienced both only means you are growing, that is if you let it mold you the right way.

Rather or not these pieces represent real love, I would have to say I love everything that every woman has taught me through it all.
Thank You

Inscriptions From The Heart

At a time when I knew nothing of true love…it seemed fate chose the person I met…a sweet pedal from the opposite sex…that showed me how hot and deep passion could get
Have you ever been so in love that your footsteps were on a layer of thin air…then if not…how can I explain the emotions that flared…when she was on my side…how my peripheral vision blurred…as she stared into my eyes…how the very blood the runs through my heart surged …as the laws of physics were defied
Three hundred and sixty degrees Is not enough geometrics to describe how my world became petrified…at the thought of living life with out her…you see I would rather run and hide…then to confide…in the thought of thinking the worst about her…because it was I who broke the trust…though I still wish for another chance…for our love to once again…become plush
But these lonely days make it hard to mend this broken heart of

mines...that feels crushed...into a thousand pieces...you see I could write a three page thesis...on how her life gives my life meaning...but it would only be demeaning...to think I didn't play a major role, that caused her heart to turn as cold ...as December...that caused our world to fold...but I pray that she remembers...the happy days...even though mental cars make it easy to track the many ways I betrayed our love

Now that I think of it, she must have been crazy to have stayed...through all the games that I played...through all the mistakes that I made...or maybe!

It was all the prayers that I prayed...that kept her from walking away

But in the end...I only deceived myself to believe she wouldn't leave because of all the jokers that I dealt

Now I am left with these Inscriptions From The Heart...

That constantly gives a vivid description...

To what led us to part.

Good Morning

I wake to inspiration; I wake to anticipation to see all the beauty of life's creations. I anxiously fumble with my pen to write about its vision hoping to capture a strong inspiring inspiration…thinking this is the right piece!
Thinking this will be someone's morning motivation…so here it is stamped with my abbreviation…hopefully it will help you thru your frustration
My message to you is simply this… Every morning you wake you are truly blessed.

Poetry

Collaboration with Poetry James
Engraved and reincarnated within my soul…she makes my wisdom seem so old…she peels back layers of understanding with metaphors that opens my mind while in a world that thinks so close minded…she brings me out of grey areas where once I was blinded…allowing my vision to see in infrared…where struggle and pain has bled…allowing me to see the tenacity and beauty in it all…I am truly thankful that she dwells with in me…this thing! We call Poetry.

<Poetry James>
When obstacles seem to overwhelm me…he brings me to a place where I only exist…to help cleanse and clear my mind by writing or reciting with words, the feelings I have inside…I use him to reveal my most intimate thoughts and desires…where the world may look confused and dismiss the words I may have used…because they don't understand this different type of language I am using…That's ok

because we have a different form of release…mine is my comfort zone My Poetry I say the least.

<Leevance Willams>

She makes me come to a place where her comfort zone is my safe haven…keeping me sane, putting me in a frame, of mind where I no longer need to complain…she stabilizes my equilibrium…keeping me balanced in a world that constantly loses its direction Giving me protection like the wings from an angel…she brings me to a Captain Kurt status…Boldly going where no man has gone before…so when I hear her name I think of a universe beyond this universe…a universe with unlimited boundaries of intellect, with love, with dialect…a place where the phrase, Comfort Zone, is no longer needed because everyone is more tightly woven then Madea's Family.

<Poetry James>

A reunion is an understatement when it comes to how he makes me feel, while in the midst of our own world of intimate passion…in which you can only

understand…after we have expressed our passion in words…we decide to go mingle and communicate with others that surrounds us… with lots of intelligent conversation and intriguing thoughts…some politics, controversies and such, every one having their own emotional glitch which sets us off yet with a loving touch. Life is full of obstacles in which we may face…in order to step over them successfully we all should have this special place.
<Leevance Willams>
A special place is where she keeps me…like when I wake in the morning…she is an extension of the process of yawning…calming me…preparing me for the ups and downs that life throws me on a day to day basis…giving me the strength to tackle my problems on a intellectual level…she helps me to understand my place my mate and all that is required to communicate…she helps me to hold my tongue when my outburst would just become belligerent…she keeps me my confidence at a level of kingship…she is my queen and she

sits beside me at all times…I guess I am constantly having a threesome because when I make love to my mate, she is constantly whispering in my ear…I wouldn't have it no other way…what more can I say!

Confused

How do I make her understand...that the sun and the moon do not co exist with out compromise?
How do I hold her hand and not show the resistance of arrogance from the persistence to be her man...how do I take a stand?...while not falling weak from the feeling of wanting to be loved
But most importantly
How do I let her know she is the only queen for me in this abundantly unpredictable filled land?

Heaven Sent

She told me good night, as she became consumed by her weary day
Needless to say…the strength that she display...could only be heaven sent
She graciously awaits for her king patiently with faith…knowing god will send him with that loving, supportive trait
She said she will know because their will be a bond that not even the devil himself could break
She said she will know because she sees him In her dreams…She believes this by all means… and know its more than just thought…she said she already loves him even though physically they are apart
It confused me for a moment and I realized…spiritually is how she keeps him in her heart.

A Letter To My Queen

Your smile brightens my day…even though we have distance as a resistance…still the existence of your words brightens my day

I have so longed awaited for a Queen of your stats…you have walked in my dreams leaving heart felt tracks, but it seemed like a life time to find you...your every stride coincides with royalty…your voice reassures me that my crown has no value with out the sparkling diamonds of your crown

Before I met you my life was just sand in the wind, an hour glass damaged…turning the hours of my days into weeks that passed like minutes…your physical form took me by storm…appearing out of no where like the clouds starting to form before the rain is born

It's funny how I can still smell your fragrance when we carefully touched each other for the first time, trying to give hugs that showed no intimate emotions…if only you knew!

You actually threw me a flotation device with your arm because I was drowning within myself…screaming for help…But, But...my damage past caused my cries to fall on deaf ears
Now here it is I'm facing my greatest fear's (screaming)
One!...one is to finally meet that soul that compliments me like corn bread does collard greens…yet I don't have the yams to show the appreciation and how sweet she is
Second! Seeing her kingdom so vast that I don't have the ruling hands to help stretch with hers and rule it
So I have to step back!
Back into a world of phony smiles because of my looks…if only they would have the intellect to really understand this man…this book
Maybe time will be so kind to allow me to grow that extension to unlock the door of my enclosed world of detention…finally giving me the chance to love my queen just as she loves me…while seeing myself just as she sees me
I was so stuck within this selfless person inside me, that I

forgot the potential that resides in me
In other words!
It felt like the first time I could see a rose and really acknowledge the beauty and tenacity of it...she gave that to me…so here is my gift to her
My heart stays in your hand, while physically staying away…until…I can…walk and help her rule…as a King…as her Man.

No Good Man

Am I an aviation pilot?
Because I can make you feel higher than an astronaut soaring through the stars…nawww, not by far, but some may call me a spiritual analyst…sending stimulations and vibrations that repeats it self in your mind like incantations
Be careful…I am deep and destructive like a detonation exploding in your mind
Am I hypnosis? By the power of my persuasion…I kid you not…I have seen cravings that they give their last all just because I ask
Am I a terrorist?
Because damn! I swear some don't know how scary it gets, to see all that you have worked for come tumbling down and crash…all because you le me in your life
Am I the senate or the IRS?
Because I make my own rules, rearranging words keeping you

confused to the fact that in the end all you think you have accumulated you will eventually lose… if it's not for me then its nothing at all
AT@T don't have my technology because my connection can never be disrupted, you come running every time I call
You should have worked for the circus as many times I have made a clown out of you
I have even been called a foreman because of the way I make blue prints to tear down your walls…reconstructing you to function for my own needs…they say if it breaths it bleeds…well last time I looked I ad no heart…so what keeps me alive?
Maybe the pleasure of tearing down your pride…using it against you…maybe the pleasure of sending you through a rough ride, separating you from those that are close to you
Fuck what you are going through and what you been through…hell! I can even use that to get your understanding…it don't matter if you are liberated, self motivated

or even high strung…eventually you will bow down
You see I no longer just hang in the ghetto these days I hang mostly downtown…watching the briefcases with careers…the stethoscopes that listen to hearts…especially the ones who paint their faces with strength but have the stench of self conscious fears
Have you guessed who I am?
Well a lot of people compare me to a drug…that indeed I am
I will give you a chance once or twice then I will take it away…I will give you the sense of freedom as I spread my deceit
Your best option is to just turn away and wash your hands...Did you guess it yet?
I am a no good man.

A Voice

The voice was familiar
The emotions that flared from its tone brought back memories of lust…it brought back images of confrontations stemmed from no trust
Even though it still sounded angelic, I had to remember what we had was some what of a relic…simply the past
Wished it would have lasted through the test of time but as we all know in life and relationship, there are no buttons for rewind
Captivated…with how this voice activated and reinstated feelings that I have suppressed that almost decapitated…my frame of mind
I must be out of my mind to even listen…I purposely made myself blind to enhance my resistance
Still I see her eyes glistening…as I picture her smile that blurs my peripheral vision to all that's around me

Unfortunately I can still feel the missing space in my heart taunting me wishing that voice would have never found me
Before it fades away into the distant of the distance that binds us…I fight to not say I love you
I must have put up a good fight because the words never escaped its prison of solitude
So I looked at the phone as it read, "Call Disconnected" and with a tear
I say…I love you.

Making Love In The Club

As the lights slowly dimmed the songstress began to sing...the room started to blur...everything began to fade giving aide to the image of just me! And Her!

We became one like Miles Davis with his trumpet...her voice singing solos to my soul...her eyes sending Morris code to my cerebellum...her body movement sent shivers down my spine...building an erotic curiosity that exploded within the thoughts of my mind

She sung to me like Jeanie in a lamp and lord knows! I wanted her to grant me a wish

She had my hunger at an all time high and her dress made her succulent skin look like a 4 star dish

The more I listened to her the more I lost myself in a moment of bliss...at one time I had to look and see if anyone saw me blowing her a kiss...SHIT! CSI could not have detected the cruel way she raped me of my heart

I took long slow strides across the floor to keep my zipper and my portabella mushroom apart...I safely made it to the bar hopping the blue top bottle could calm that intoxicating aphrodisiac she blew in my ears...but the ramifications was less then the exaggeration of mixing fire with gasoline
What I mean is the more I saturated my thirst the more saturated I became
Her session was over and I heard her walking towards me through the thick haze of game spitting brother shot in her direction...I began to feel two different erections, of course the one that stood out was the intense curiosity to make love to her mind
She sat next to me and gave me orgasm after orgasm
She spoke of blackness
She spoke of black men
She spoke of black heritage
She spoke of black love
I lit me a cigarette and she took it from my lips...toked it and gave it back and with a twist...she pecked me with her lips and simply said...imagination may be left to

the mind but making love happens all the time and people never notice it
I watched her walk away and realized...with out a touch of a hand...I had been...MADE LOVE TO IN A CLUB.

CHAPTER FIVE

Thankful

Through my journey I have thought about my kids on so many occasions, while at the same time thinking of my father who was never there. As parents we want to be the best we can, sometimes we fall short in areas. I am not perfect nor do I portray to be but I pray I can be a better parent than my father was. I love you Albert Antoine, Leevance Williams Jr and Jada Milord. In this chapter I pay homage to my mother, kids and give thanks for simply making it this far.

A Father's Selfish Ways

I sit here thinking of all my plans and dreams and how real all of them seemed…but never quite transpired

The looks on my children's face…every time I was filed in a judicial case…how incarceration made me out of a liar

A woman once told me, "Take care of your kids and watch how your world would unfold".

Spent days in a cell praying and wishing

Fought through a haze of drug addiction

Stood strong through a stint of homeless affliction…but never put myself in the frame of mind…to test that theory to see if her words were lame or blind

So I found myself sometimes in a state of depression…because my life was out of order

If I tackled one and prevailed…the neglecting of another would make it seemed as if I still

failed…they say Rome was not built in a day…but tell that to your kids when a summer spent, was their stomachs' clinched…from eating oodles of noodles
I find myself digging up skeletons trying to find the part of me that passed away
Wishing
I never would have dug through the debris still ending up with no solutions…just empty resolutions, still gazing out of correctional institutions
Most importantly still falling short of a father's responsibility to his children's restitution
But as I dug deeper I found more respect for the love of my children through the memory of my fatherless days…
Ya see a mother and son's love is a different type of phase…so with that!!
I hope to break that cycle of
A Father Selfish Ways.

Those Eyes

Every time I close my eyes
I see your eyes open up…just like an over filled cup…I see them over flowing…they are shape like hers but look like mine…I would have loved to watch them mature over time
I was so in love with this Pocahontas spirit...we made love deep and hard…that she was able to penetrate the china brick wall that surrounded my heart
Passion turned into life with in life…then her irreconcilable actions came crashing down with all of its might
The subject of her words…crumbled and cracked, making it hard to announce
But my verbs…stood strong for my culture and seed as they were pronounced
Unfortunately her soul was so tainted that the thought of her action was easily denounced
The exchange for currency, to keep the same frame of life

currently….didn't sit to well as I thought about my first encounter with the nightmares of premature eyes
Eyes that still cry in my dreams
That love turned into hate…that passion turned into disgust…the sweet quiet times turned into…HUSH BITCH BEFORE I BUST YOU IN YOUR MOUTH
Now I am left with the shame…the what ifs and the nightmares
Every time I close my eyes
I see your eyes open up…just like an over filled cup…I see them over flowing…they are shape like hers but look like mine…I would have loved to watch them mature over time.

What Would It Have Been Like

Coming up as a child I had a vivid and wild imagination…but I had no clue how to grasp hold and make sense of the hole that he left in my soul

I tried not to show no disrespect to any of the woman who raised me with love and no regrets…but little did I know as my feet got bigger and my chest got thicker…I was still left pondering and wondering

What Would It Have Been Like

Many days I tried to decipher if a child's birth is so beautiful and great…then why was my birth so belittled to this date...That he was shame to stay and let my vision mature enough to see his face

I watched as other kids were guided and enjoyed their own…but if I would have known… what I knew now, then maybe I wouldn't have felt so disowned, and not have to pretend that my pain was so well endowed

I went through many trials none the fault of my dear mother…she gave me love and affection, trust and acceptance…consoling hugs through out my years of rebellions, she even taught me to understand my blessings

Yet and still I found myself staring out the window of life, Guessing…What Would It Have Been Like

I played more than my part, got his number and called…a 10 minute conversation that left me confused, hurt and appalled…I left my number be the stranger never called

The world seemed even colder because I was filled with his blood and posses his biological DNA

I look in the mirror and I look and see the unsatisfactory of my own actions…the caption in bold letters of dissatisfactory in my own kids face…a legacy I dread to leave them

Wondering…What Would It Have Been Like If I was There

Dear Mama

I applauded my mother, always staying on track…always breaking her back to provide…in fact! Many days she lied about the pain that it took to satisfy the look and needs in her sons eyes…the word tried…she broke it in half because every obstacle was defied when it came to home…making a living for us sometimes meant her leaving us alone…but don't get it twisted with society's justification because there was always emergency instructions do to a strong connection…much affection…there were never a time we felt rejection

HELL! My first black election was way before Obama…because no one could rule my world better than my Dear Mama

As I grew up hell yeah there was drama, mostly because my black ass thought I knew it all…I wish I knew then what I know now then maybe I could have avoided the

many times I set myself up for a downfall
She taught me how to stand tall, She taught me just because you are broke don't mean you have to look like it, always saying, "If you need me just call".
Through drugs, crime and lies I lost that loving hand she gave me…there were many times I didn't deserve the hand she lent just to save me
Through the years my middle name became drama…but yet and still besides the dear lord,
No one was there…but…My Dear Mama.

Good Morning

I wake to inspiration,
I wake to the anticipation to see all the beauty of life's creation,
I anxiously fumble with my pen to write about its vision hoping to capture a strong inspiring translation,
Thinking this piece right here! Will be someone's morning motivation, so here it is stamped with my abbreviation,
Hopefully it helps you thru your frustration,
When you wake every morning and able to take a deep breath and try it all over again…You! Are! Truly Blessed!

It Lives With In Me
No matter how hard it gets, I hold my guard, kneel and pray by starting off with this,
"Our Father Who Art in Heaven", you know the rest…and I must confess it keeps me grounded…Then I pick my pen and paper up and began to write…to some their brains become confounded…but it frees me every since I found it,
Different phrases describing different phases, of my life…it may leave some people dumbfounded all because the way it sounded,
But open your mind, free the shackles that hold it confined with no key...it allows me to understand life by tapping into the reason for…the reason why and the question how,
Did I lose you?
Wipe your eyes…clear the wool that blurs your vision…these words won't be shown on your television…but they will damn sure make an incision into your mind if

you let it...not just because I!
Said it
But because knowledge is power...some people bring words together but this shit right here!!!
It brings people together
It gives me relief
It gives me hope
It gives me drive and it feeds my soul...this wonderful and beautiful thing we call poetry.

One To Grow On

As I stroll through this universe we call life…dealing with these pains and strife, these wrongs and rights, I see they are much like…tumble weeds that blows in the wind…they are back and forth again and again

So to keep my mentality…I face reality upon the battlefield equipped with knowledge for armor and steal but of course reinforced with courage and strong will

Sometimes I see myself stumbling and eventually I fall…but from what I recall…I dust myself off and again I stand tall

Because you see pot holes and obstacles are meant to be put in our path like questions are meant to be asked…to give a clear and better view and an appreciation much stronger and true

But many of us fail to understand…that the world has already been placed in our hands…its just up to us to look through every grain of sand and lead and cultivate this land

And to me!
That is the only way to become a man.

Thank You

I exhale as the sun sets the scene to the end of another day…I gather my thoughts to bow my head and pray…Fixate myself into a quiet calm place and this is what I say…Dear lord I thank you for ranting me the opportunities you have sent my way…Didn't know how I was going to have an income but still I kept the faith,
Stress invaded my mind with unbelievable weight, over flowing my plate
But you knew my appetite so I just absorbed it all…… like nourishment…you sent angels to whisper words of encouragement…now I stand strong as a red wood tree in storm…smiling..I thank you.

The End

I open my eyes today and say… Thank you…Thank you for holding me…and even though knowingly, I may fall again
I know you'll help me stand tall again…its hard to walk these streets and not call it a sin…but I still se my growth and I hope I can look back at that walk and be proud before you call it the end

www.ingramcontent.com/pod-product-compliance
Lightning Source LLC
Chambersburg PA
CBHW031255290426
44109CB00012B/592